PEOPLE WHO HELP US

POLICE OFFICER

Rebecca Hunter

**Photography by
Chris Fairclough**

CHERRYTREE BOOKS

A Cherrytree book

Reprinted in 2006
Evans Brothers Ltd
2A Portman Mansions
Chiltern Street
London W1U 6NR

British Library Cataloguing in Publication Data
Hunter, Rebecca
  Police Officer. - (People who help us)
  1. Physicians - Juvenile literature
  I. Title
  363. 2'2
© Evans Brothers Ltd 2005

ISBN 1-84234299-1
13 digit ISBN (from 1 January 2007) 9781842342992

Planned and produced by Discovery Books Ltd
Editor: Rebecca Hunter
Designer: Ian Winton

Acknowledgements
Photograph on p19 (top) reproduced with kind permission of the Merseyside Police.
All other photography by Chris Fairclough.

The author, packager and publisher would like to thank the following people for their participation in the
book: PC Sam Jennings, Julie Farnsworth, PC Phil Smith, PC Bob Austin, PC Richard Whates and all the
other officers of Merseyside Police Liverpool South; Julie Gornell and the young people from Penny Lane
Development Trust; and Year 2 and the teachers of King David Infant School, Liverpool.

Models were used for the crime scenes on pages 16–18 in this book.

Words appearing in bold **like this**, are explained in the glossary.

Contents

I am a police officer

My name is Sam. I am a police officer.

I am a Police Constable with Merseyside Police in Liverpool.

I work here at Allerton Police Station.

A police officer has many different jobs to do. I have to try to prevent **crimes**, catch **criminals** and generally help people in the community.

Morning parade

8.00 I arrive at the police station. Some of the officers are already leaving for their day's work. This is Dave on his motorbike. He is going out to monitor the traffic and to try to stop people driving too fast.

I go to my locker to fetch my uniform and equipment.

Then I go to our morning parade meeting. Inspector Fox tells us what we will be doing today.

Checking equipment

Before I go out I put on the rest of my uniform – my **body armour** and my equipment belt.

This is my hat. It is very hard to protect my head.

hat

ID badge

Here are some of the other things I use.

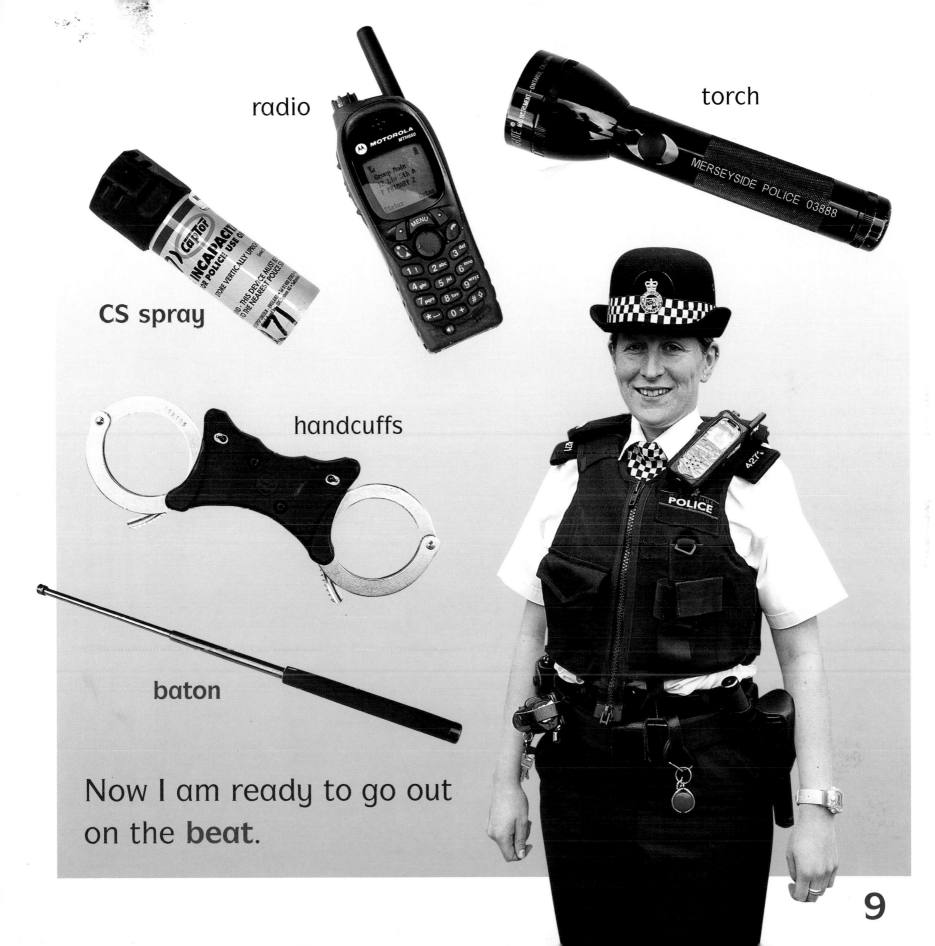

radio

torch

CS spray

handcuffs

baton

Now I am ready to go out on the **beat**.

9

On the beat

This morning I start my beat down at the Albert Dock. I walk along beside the river.

Normally it is very busy here with lots of visitors taking ferry boat rides. But it is raining today, and there are not many people about.

I stop and talk to a man and his little boy. It is nice to be able to chat to people and answer their questions.

A **tourist** asks me for directions. She shows me where she wants to go on her map, and I show her the quickest way.

Radio call

Later in the morning I walk up to the high street. It is busier here. Lots of people are out doing their shopping.

I get a call on my radio. I have to **investigate** an incident.

This man has just found that his wall is covered with **graffiti**. He is very cross. It has happened before. Graffiti is very expensive to clean off. I tell him we will try to catch whoever is responsible.

Lunchtime

12.30 It is time for lunch. I bought a sandwich in town earlier, and I take it to the restroom. Bob, another officer, is also eating his lunch here.

After lunch, I have to spend some time on the front desk.

This is where people come to report things to the police.

These boys are reporting the **theft** of a mobile phone. I take down all the details.

An **emergency** 999 call has just come in.
A shopkeeper has caught some boys
shoplifting. We must go there straight
away. I need another officer to help me so
I take Richard with me. We run to the van.

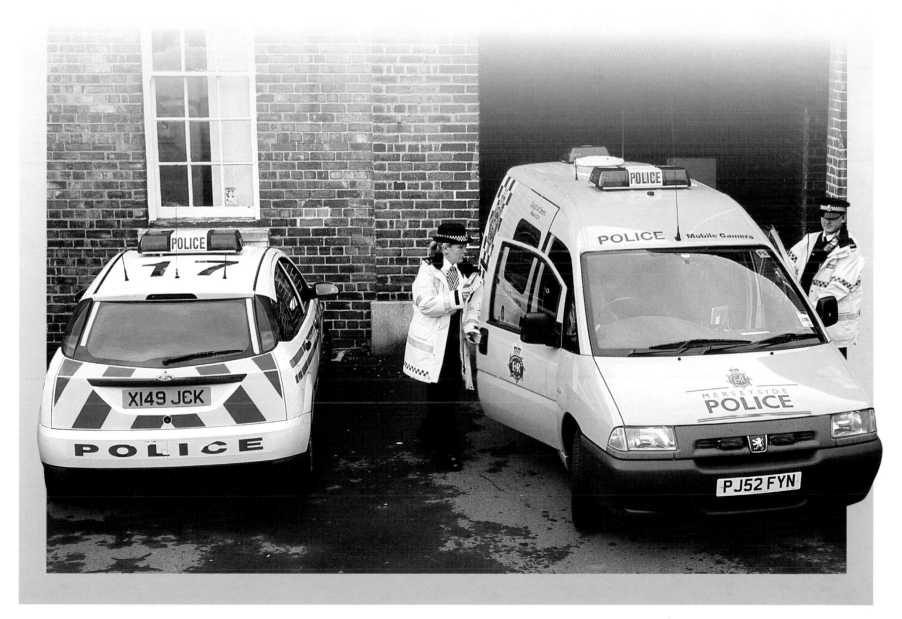

Call-out

We go to the shop in the high street.
It is a chemist. The shopkeeper saw
the boys putting things into a bag.
They were not going to pay for them.

I write down the shopkeeper's name and address and the details of what the boys tried to steal.

The boys are **arrested**.

They will have to come back to the police station with us.

Under arrest

We put the boys in the back of the van.

When we get back to the police station I ring the boys' parents and ask them to come to the police station.

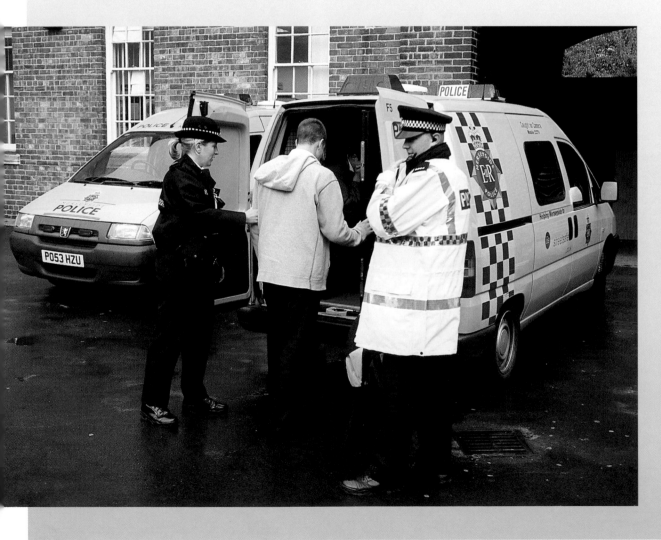

The boys will have to go to **court** where a **judge** will decide what punishment to give them. They may have to go to prison.

We take their **fingerprints**.

I go to my office. I have to write up all that has happened today on my computer.

School visit

Police officers often visit schools.
We have many things to tell children,
including how to stay safe and how
to make an emergency phone call.

Today I visit King David's School. I talk to the children about the dangers of fireworks, since it is Bonfire Night soon.

The children are very keen to answer my questions.

I make sure they know the basic firework code.

Before I leave the school, I put up some firework posters.

The police service

It is hard work being a police officer but I do enjoy my job.

I get to meet lots of people and help make their lives better by catching criminals.

The police officers I work with are friendly and always happy to help people in trouble.

Glossary

arrest to stop and take someone to a police station because it is believed they have committed a crime

baton a short stick used by police officers to defend themselves

beat the route that a police officer follows each day

body armour clothing that protects the body

court a place where legal matters are decided by a judge

crime an action for which you can be punished

criminal a person who commits a crime

CS spray a spray used to 'stun' or 'stop' someone. Used to protect others and defend police officers.

emergency a serious situation that must be dealt with immediately

fingerprints the marks made by the tips of your fingers. The fingers can be dipped in ink or scanned by a computer.

graffiti writing or drawings that are scribbled on walls

ID badge short for 'identification' badge. The police have to carry one to show who they are.

investigate to find out something

judge the person in a law court who decides how criminals should be punished

shoplifting stealing things from a shop

theft the action of stealing something

tourist someone who is on holiday

Index